I Am King!

Written by Mary Packard

Illustrated by Leonid Gore

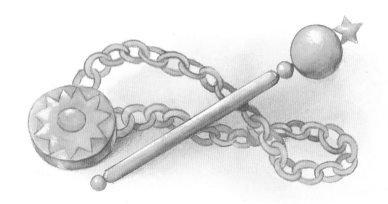

My First READER

children's press®

A Division of Scholastic Inc.
New York Toronto London Auckland Sydney
Mexico City New Delhi Hong Kong
Danbury, Connecticut

Library of Congress Cataloging-in-Publication Data

Packard, Mary.
 I am king! / written by Mary Packard ; illustrated by Leonid Gore.–
[1st American ed.].
      p. cm. – (My first reader)
Summary: A little boy pretends that he is king of everything, commanding
his army.
 ISBN 0-516-22927-3 (lib. pbk.)   0-516-24629-1 (pbk.)
 [1. Imagination–Fiction. 2. Kings, queens, rulers, etc.–Fiction. 3.
Stories in rhyme.] I. Gore, Leonid, ill. II. Title. III. Series.
 PZ8.3.P125Iab 2003
 [E]–dc21
                                        2003003632

3 4 5 6 7 8 9 10 R 12 11 10 09 08 07   62

Note to Parents and Teachers

Once a reader can recognize and identify the 35 words
used to tell this story, he or she will be able to read successfully the
entire book. These 35 words are repeated throughout the story, so that
young readers will be able to easily recognize
the words and understand their meaning.

The 35 words used in this book are:

ahead	drum	look	send
am	everything	march	soldiers
and	flag	my	the
army	get	of	they
as	go	on	to
bed	hear	ring	trumpets
come	here	run	way
crown	I	say	your
do	king	see	

I am king.

Do as I say!

Soldiers march!

Go on your way!

See my crown?

See my ring?

I am king of everything!

Hear the trumpets.

Hear the drum.

See the flag.

Here they come!

Get your trumpets, flag, and drum!

Send the army on the run!

Come on, soldiers.

Look ahead!

Come on, king.

Go to bed!

ABOUT THE AUTHOR

Mary Packard has been writing children's books for as long as she can remember. Packard lives in Northport, New York, with her family. Besides writing, she loves music, theater, animals, and, of course, children of all ages.

ABOUT THE ILLUSTRATOR

Leonid Gore was born in Minsk, USSR. After he graduated from the Art Institute in Minsk, he worked as an illustrator for various book, magazine, and newspaper publishers. In 1991, Gore and his wife, Nina, immigrated to the United States. They now live in Oakland, New Jersey, with their daughter, Emily.